Copyright © 1984, 1988 by Annette Tison & Talus Taylor.
English translation © 1989 by Annette Tison & Talus Taylor.
All rights reserved.
First published in the United States of America
in 1989 by Grosset & Dunlap, Inc.,
a member of The Putnam Publishing Group, New York.
Printed in Spain. Published simultaneously in Canada.
Library of Congress Catalog Card Number: 88-82185
ISBN 0-448-21552-7   A B C D E F G H I J

(Portions of this book originally appeared in
THE BIG BOOK OF ANIMAL RECORDS.)
Artes Gráficas Toledo, S.A.
D.L.TO:2458-1988

ANIMALS LARGE AND SMALL

Annette Tison & Talus Taylor

Publishers · **Grosset & Dunlap** · *New York*

TABLE OF
CONTENTS

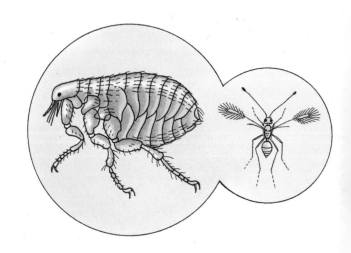

Since it is not possible in most cases to illustrate the animals at their actual size—some being invisible without a microscope and others being far too large for the page—we have tried, where possible, to give an idea of the scale by including pictures of such familiar animals as cats, cows, mice, fleas, and humans.

Mammals

Scientists have divided the animal kingdom into a certain number of classes, from the simplest creatures to the most complex—from one-celled protozoans to mammals. We have decided to start this book with the latter because humans belong to this class.

All-time biggest

The biggest animal living today—and the biggest that ever lived—is the female blue whale. Unlike most mammals, the male blue whale is smaller than the female, by 6 percent. At an average of about 143 tons (130 tonnes), the enormous whale weighs as much as 4 brontosaurs, or 20 elephants, or 180 cows, or 1,600 men.

In 1947 a 209-ton (190-tonne) female blue whale was caught! Her heart weighted 990 lb (450 kg); her spine 15,400 lb (7,000 kg); her tongue 6,600 lb (3,000 kg); and her brain 18.3 lb (8.3 kg).

Although the female blue whale is the heaviest animal, she may not be the longest. At 110 ft (33.6 m), she falls far short of a giant sea worm reported at 180 ft (55 m). (See chapter on invertebrates.)

blue whale

blue whale calf

Pretty baby

At birth a blue whale calf weighs about 4,440 lb (2,000 kg) and measures 23 ft (7 m) in length. The mother nurses her baby, as other mammals do. The little one fills out nicely. Every day it puts on about 440 lb (200 kg) and grows almost 1¼ in. (3 cm).

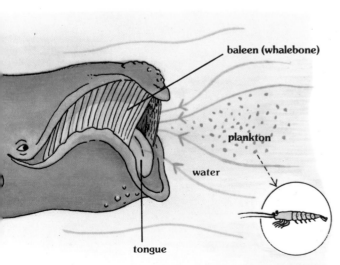

baleen (whalebone)

plankton

water

tongue

Whale groups

There are two major groups of whales: the baleen whales and the toothed whales. The blue whale is a baleen whale. Instead of teeth, it has an upper jaw of horny plates called baleen, or whalebone. This allows the whale to filter the plankton—tiny crustaceans (shrimplike creatures) and microscopic algae (seaweed)—that it eats. A blue whale can eat 8,800 lb (4,000 kg) of plankton a day.

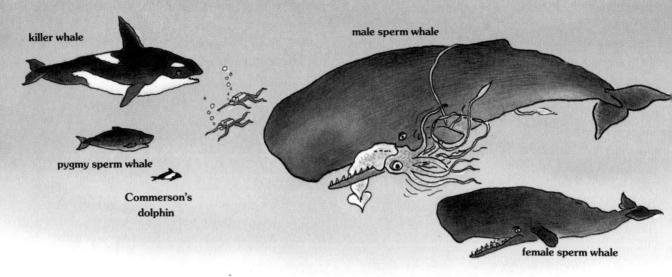

killer whale

male sperm whale

pygmy sperm whale

Commerson's
dolphin

female sperm whale

More sea mammals

The largest toothed whale is the male sperm whale, with a length of 66 ft (20 m) and a weight of 55 tons (50 tonnes). The male is about twice as large as the female.

The smallest toothed whale is the pygmy sperm whale, which measures only 13 ft (4 m).

Dolphins are toothed whales. The largest one, the ferocious killer whale, grows up to 31 ft (9.5 m) and weighs up to 5½ tons (5 tonnes). Killer whales hunt together and do not hesitate to attack whales bigger than themselves.

The smallest sea mammal is Commerson's dolphin, at 4 ft (1.2 m) and 50 lb (23 kg).

Whale hunting

Whale hunting has been going on since prehistoric times. When it was a craft, the whale population was not threatened. But modern techniques have brought some kinds of whales nearly to extinction.

whale hunting, from a 19th-century engraving

Heavyweight land animals

The gold medal goes to the African elephant. The biggest males weigh more than 8 tons (7.5 tonnes) and measure 13 ft (4 m) high and nearly 30 ft (9 m) from the tip of the trunk to the tip of the tail. The Asiatic elephant is smaller, at 5½ tons (5 tonnes) and nearly 10 ft (3 m) high.

The heaviest ungulate—hoofed mammal—is the square-lipped rhinoceros of Africa, whose average weight is between 3¼ and 4½ tons (3-4 tonnes), but which can weigh 5½ tons (5 tonnes).

The river hippopotamus, which also lives in Africa, can weigh up to 4½ tons (4 tonnes). Among hippos, it is quite possible to confuse the pygmy hippopotamus with a baby hippopotamus.

African elephant

Masai giraffe

square-lipped rhinoceros

river hippopotamus

pygmy hippopotamus

The tallest animal

An elephant standing on its hind legs with its trunk up can reach leaves 28 ft (8.5 m) high. But the Masai giraffe is the tallest animal in its normal standing position—nearly 20 feet (6 m) to the tip of its horns. Its legs are so long that the giraffe must spread them like scissors in order to drink, despite its long neck.

From the smallest to the largest

1. Savi's pygmy shrew: 0.07 oz (2 g)
2. Cat: 9 lb (4 kg)
3. Pig: 400 lb (180 kg)
4. Cow: 1,500 lb (700 kg)
5. Indian rhinoceros: 6,600 lb (3,000 kg)
6. River hippopotamus: 8,800 lb (4,000 kg)
7. African elephant: 15,400 lb (7,000 kg)
8. Blue whale: 286,000 lb (130,00 kg)

Kodiak, or Alaskan brown bear

Derby eland

lesser Malay mouse deer

least weasel

Siberian tiger

royal antelope

Salt's dik-dik

domestic cat

African black-footed cat

Antelopes and other ruminants—cud chewers

The largest antelope, the Derby eland of Africa, can weigh up to 2,200 lb (1,000 kg). The biggest males can be 6½ ft (2 m) high at the shoulder.

The smallest antelopes are the royal antelope, with a height of 10 in. (25 cm) and a weight of 8 lb (3.6 kg), and Salt's dik-dik, which at 6½ lb (3 kg) and 14 in. (35 cm) is lighter but taller. Both of these antelopes also live in Africa.

The smallest ruminant fits on one hand. The lesser Malay mouse deer is 8 in. (20 cm) tall, 18 in. (45 cm) long, and weighs 4½ lb (2 kg). The canine teeth of the males look a bit like Dracula's, but this shy animal feeds mainly on herbs and fruit.

Carnivores—meat eaters

The biggest carnivores are bears—the Kodiak, or Alaskan brown bear, and the polar bear. Both can weigh up to 2,200 lb (1,000 kg). Standing on its hind legs, the Kodiak is almost 10 feet (3 m) tall.

The smallest carnivores are two forms of the least weasel of Europe. Adults of these animals weigh no more than 1¼ oz (35 g) and measure 6½ in. (16 cm), tail included.

Cats

The biggest cat is the Siberian tiger. It can measure up to 11½ ft (3.5 m) from the tip of its nose to the tip of its tail, and it can weigh almost 850 lb (380 kg).

The smallest cat is the African black-footed cat. Much smaller than the domestic cat, it is only about 20 in. (50 cm) long from its nose to the tip of its tail.

male

female

southern elephant seals

Male and female

We call the differences in size and appearance between the males and females of the same animal "sexual dimorphism." In mammals the males are usually larger, and they sometimes have special body adornments, such as horns, tusks, beards, or manes.

The biggest difference in weight between males and females of the same mammal is found among the southern elephant seals of Antarctica. Males weigh four times as much as females, about 8,400 lb (3,800 kg). The male, which has a short trunk over its forehead, fights his rivals in order to win the female. Elephant seals are the largest pinnipeds—flippered animals such as walruses, and seals.

The long and short of it

Major size differences can occur also between examples of the same kind of animal of the same sex. For example, a man 5 ft 3 in. (1.6 m) tall is considered normal, and so is one 6 ft 7 in. (2 m). In dogs, these individual differences have reached ridiculous proportions because of breeding. A Great Dane can, in theory, breed with a Chihuahua.

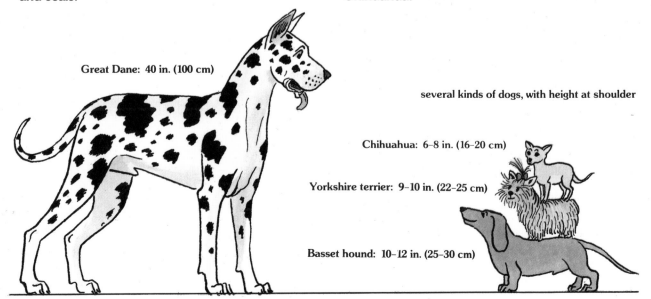

Great Dane: 40 in. (100 cm)

several kinds of dogs, with height at shoulder

Chihuahua: 6–8 in. (16–20 cm)

Yorkshire terrier: 9–10 in. (22–25 cm)

Basset hound: 10–12 in. (25–30 cm)

Primates

Primates include humans, apes, monkeys, and related animals. The largest primate is the male mountain gorilla of Africa. In his normal position, with legs slightly bent, he stands 5 ft 9 in. tall (1.75 m). But if he straightened his legs, he would be 7½ ft (2.3 m) tall! He weighs up to 600 lb (275 kg) in the wild and has reached 770 lb (350 kg) in captivity. Up to the age of eight or nine, males and females are the same size. But males continue to grow for another three years, until they are twice as heavy as females.

Marsupials—pouched animals

The biggest marsupial is the red kangaroo of Australia. Its head and body measure up to 5 ft 3 in. (160 cm), and its tail can be 42 in. (105 cm) long. Upright, in a threatening pose, it stands more than 6½ ft (2 m) high.

Flying mammals

With a head-and-body length of 18 in. (45 cm), a wingspan of 63 in. (160 cm), and a weight of 3⅓ lb (1.5 kg), the fruit bat—or flying fox—of Asia is the largest flying mammal.

Rodents—gnawing mammals

The largest rodent is the capybara, or water pig, of South America. With its 20-in. (50-cm) shoulder height and weight of up to 130 lb (60 kg), it has the size and appearance of a small pig.

The harvest mouse of Europe is one of the smallest rodents, with a length, including its tail, of 4⅓ in. (11 cm) and a weight of 0.28 oz (8 g).

fruit bat

mountain gorilla

red kangaroo

capybara

harvest mouse

The smallest mammals

The smallest flying mammal is the tiny pipistrelle, an African dwarf insect-eating bat. Weight: 0.09 oz (2.5 g); length of head and trunk: 1½ in. (3.8 cm). Kitti's hog-nosed bat of Thailand is of a similar size.

The smallest land mammal is Savi's pygmy shrew of Europe. Weight: 0.07 oz (2 g); length of head and trunk: 1½ in. (4 cm); tail: 1 in. (2.5 cm).

The smallest marsupial is the Kimberley planigale of Australia. Weight: 0.18 oz (5 g); length of head and trunk: 2⅜ in. (6 cm); tail: 2 in. (5 cm).

The smallest monkey is the pygmy marmoset of South America. Weight: 2½ oz (70 g); length of head and trunk: 6¼ in. (16 cm); tail: 7 in. (18 cm).

The smallest primate is the lesser mouse lemur of Madagascar. Weight: 1¾ oz (50 g); length of head and trunk: 4⅓ in. (11 cm); tail: 6 in. (15 cm).

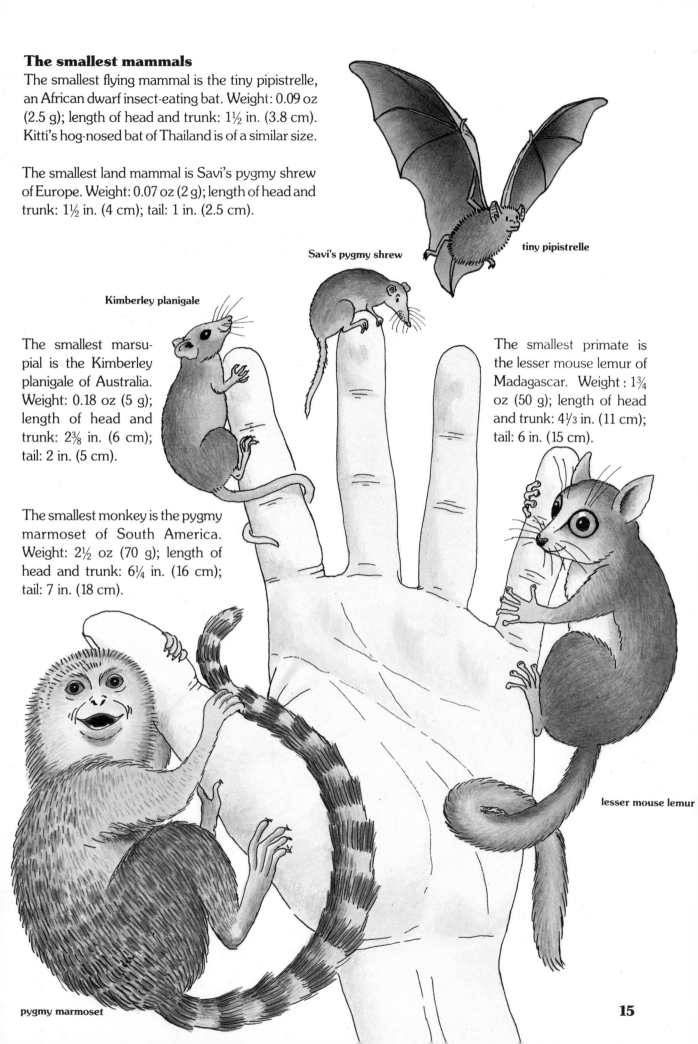

tiny pipistrelle

Savi's pygmy shrew

Kimberley planigale

lesser mouse lemur

pygmy marmoset

More small mammals

INSECT EATERS (Europe)
1. Savi's pygmy shrew: 0.07 oz (2 g)
2. Lesser shrew: 0.14 oz (4 g)
3. Alpine shrew: 0.56 oz (16 g)

RODENTS
4. Harvest mouse, Europe: 0.28 oz (8 g)
5. Northern birch mouse, Europe: 0.35 oz (10 g)
6. House mouse, worldwide: 0.60 oz (17 g)
7. Wood mouse, Europe, Asia: 0.63 oz (18 g)

MARSUPIALS (AUSTRALIA)
8. Kimberley planigale: 0.18 oz (5 g)
9. Pygmy gliding possum: 0.42 oz (12 g)
10. Thick-tailed dormouse possum: 0.53 oz (15 g)

Birds

Birds are warm-blooded vertebrates (animals with backbones) covered with feathers. They have wings but some cannot fly. Their weight varies from 330 lb (150 kg) to 0.06 oz (1.6 g).

Ratites large and small

The biggest bird in the world is the ostrich of Africa. Its head reaches nearly 10 ft (3 m) from the ground at the end of a long neck, and it can weigh 330 lb (150 kg). The ostrich's wings are useless for flying, like those of such other flightless birds, or ratites, as emus, rheas, and cassowaries.

The smallest ratite is the kiwi of New Zealand. There are kiwis the size of a small domestic hen, about 1 ft (30 cm) tall and weighing 3–4 lb (1.3–1.8 kg). But a kiwi's egg can weigh as much as 25 percent of the adult bird's weight!

The ostrich lays the biggest eggs of any bird—7 in. (18 cm), and 3⅓ lb (1.5 kg). But they are also the smallest eggs in comparison to the adult bird's weight.

The smallest flightless bird

The smallest bird that cannot fly is the Inaccessible Island rail from the islands of Tristan da Cunha in the South Atlantic Ocean. It is about 6¼ in. (16 cm) long.

Thousands of years ago it came from South America. Because it has no enemies on the island, it lost the need, and the ability, to fly.

The biggest sea bird

The emperor penguin from Antarctica holds this record at 4 ft (1.2 m) and 88 lb (40 kg). It cannot fly but is a good swimmer.

The heaviest flying bird

This record is a toss-up between the mute swan of Europe and the great bustard of Europe and Asia. They both can weigh up to 48–49 lb (22 kg).

mute swan

ostrich

domestic hen

kiwi

Inaccessible Island rail

emperor penguin

pygmy parrot

bee hummingbird

firecrest

elf owl

Eurasian robin

Small and smallest

The smallest birds are the hummingbirds. The tiniest of them, the bee hummingbird from Cuba, measures 2–2½ in. (5–6 cm) from its beak to its tail and weighs 0.06 oz (1.6 g). Its egg weighs 0.02 oz (0.5 g), almost one-third of the adult's weight—proportionately huge!

The smallest parrot, the pygmy parrot from New Guinea, measures just over 3 in. (8 cm).

The smallest European bird is the firecrest, also just over 3 in. (8 cm).

The smallest bird of prey is the elf owl of the U.S. and Mexico, at just over 5 in. (13 cm).

To give you an idea of the size of these birds, we have drawn next to them a Eurasian robin, just over 5 in. (13 cm.) long.

Wingspans

The bird with the largest wingspan—12 to 13 ft (3.65–4 m)—is the wandering albatross. Very agile in the air and on water, this elegant glider walks awkwardly and takes flight with difficulty, pedaling on the water.

Among land birds, those with the largest wingspans are the Andean condor and the lesser marabou (see pages 20–21).

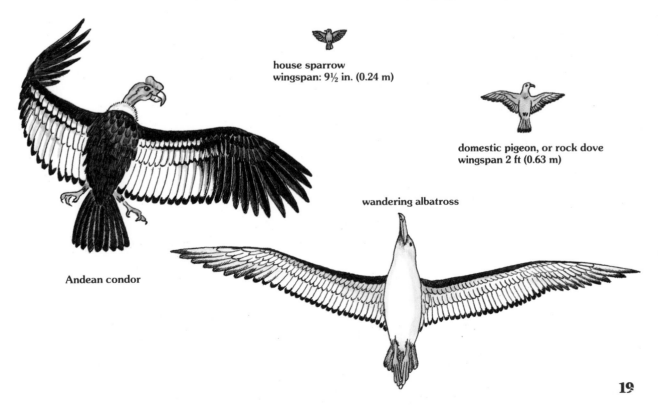

house sparrow
wingspan: 9½ in. (0.24 m)

domestic pigeon, or rock dove
wingspan 2 ft (0.63 m)

wandering albatross

Andean condor

The largest wingspans

1. Wandering albatross: 12 ft (3.65 m)
2. Andean condor: 10 ft 6 in. (3.2 m)
3. Lesser marabou: 10 ft 6 in. (3.2 m)
4. California condor: 9 ft 10 in. (3 m)
5. Eastern white pelican: 9 ft 10 in. (3 m)
6. European black vulture: 9 ft 10 in. (3 m)
7. Steller's sea eagle: 9 ft 2 in. (2.8 m)
8. Whooper swan: 8 ft 2 in. (2.5 m)
9. Golden eagle: 8 ft 2 in. (2.5 m)
10. Common crane: 7 ft 10 in. (2.4 m)
11. Magnificent frigatebird: 7 ft 6 in. (2.3 m)
12. Secretary bird: 6 ft 11 in. (2.1 m)
13. Brown pelican: 6 ft 7 in. (2 m)
14. Blue-footed booby: 4 ft 11 in. (1.5 m)

Reptiles

Reptiles are vertebrates that are covered with scales and are cold-blooded—their body temperature changes with the outside temperature. They are a varied group—lizards, turtles, snakes—and their weight varies from 4,400 lb (200 kg) to 0.07 oz (2 g).

The largest reptile

The biggest reptile of all is the giant saltwater crocodile. It can reach a length of 26¼ ft (8 m)— some say 33 ft (10 m)—and a weight of 4,400 lb (2,000 kg). It lives along beaches and in estuaries (river outlets) from the east coast of India to the Philippines and northern Australia. It can live in freshwater as well as saltwater and is sometimes found more than 550 miles (900 km) from the coast. The saltwater crocodile is greatly feared by people in the area where it lives, for it is held responsible for many accidental deaths. The Nile crocodile of Africa is somewhat smaller, but large enough at 22 ft (6.7 m).

saltwater crocodile

Komodo dragon

The biggest lizard

The Komodo dragon holds this record, with a length of 11½ ft (3.5 m) and a weight of 363 lb (165 kg). It is found only on islands in the Sunda Archipelago, mostly on Komodo Island, where it was discovered in 1911. In spite of its fierce look, the dragon is really quite tame. One of them, which lived at the Berlin Aquarium, used to follow its keeper around the grounds among the visitors.

reticulated python

king cobra

anaconda

The longest snakes

It is difficult to measure the length of a snake accurately, since when it is alive it never lies down at full length, and when dead can be stretched. When it is preserved after death, it shrinks. So there is much disagreement over the lengths of snakes.

The longest snake appears to be the reticulated python of Asia, with a record length of 32 ft 9½ in. (10 m). The anaconda of South America is slightly shorter, with a length of 29 ft 6 in. (9 m), but it is heavier. People have talked of anacondas measuring more than 46 ft (14 m), but no one has ever collected the $5,000 reward offered by the New York Zoological Society to anyone who would bring in a living snake over 30 ft long.

The longest poisonous snake is the king cobra of Asia, with a length of almost 20 ft (6 m). Its venom is strong enough to kill an elephant.

The biggest and the smallest turtles

The biggest turtle is the leatherback. It can weigh more than 1,800 lb (over 800 kg) and measure more than 8 ft (2.5 m) in length. It lives in the high seas and eats algae and fish.

The biggest land turtle is the Aldabra giant tortoise, which weighs up to 550 lb and whose shell can be 5 ft (1.5 m) long.

The biggest freshwater turtle is the alligator snapping turtle of the U.S., which can weigh 220 lb (100 kg) and whose shell reaches 31 in. (79 cm). To feed itself, this huge creature hides at the bottom of a pond and opens its mouth, which is black. At the back of the mouth is a small red piece that looks like a worm. When a smaller animal attracted to the "worm," enters the turtle's mouth, it is gobbled up.

The smallest turtle appears to be the freshwater striped mud turtle from Central America, whose shell is 3–4¾ in. (7.5–12 cm) long. The common musk tortoise of the U.S. is also very small, 3⅛–5⅛ in. (8–13 cm) long. It gives out such a bad smell that fisherman have nicknamed it the stinkpot.

leatherback

Aldabra giant tortoise

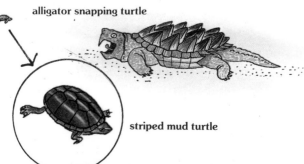

alligator snapping turtle

striped mud turtle

Strange and scaly

The green vine snake from South America is long and thin. This threadlike snake, 6½ ft (2 m) long and ½ in. (1.25 cm) thick, can be mistaken for the tropical vines among which it moves freely.

The Javan wart snake is fat and wrinkled. It slithers through the water in search of fish.

The pancake tortoise of Africa is flat and soft. It has a flexible shell 1–1¼ in. (3 cm) thick. When frightened, it hides in the crack of a rock and inflates its lungs so that it cannot be moved out.

green vine snake

Javan wart snake

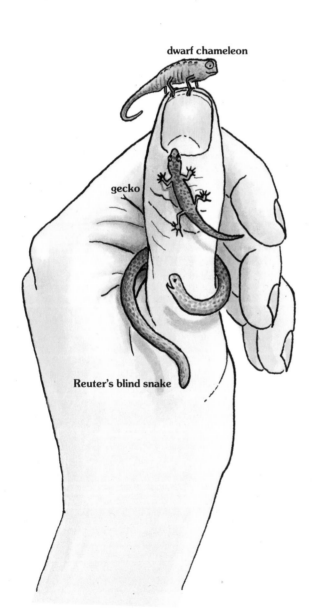
dwarf chameleon
gecko
Reuter's blind snake

pancake tortoise

The smallest reptiles

The smallest reptile is a tiny lizard called a gecko. It measures 1–1½ in. (3–4 cm) and weighs about 0.07 oz (2 g).

The dwarf chameleon from Madagascar is not any longer but is probably heavier.

The smallest snake seems to be Reuter's blind snake, which grows no longer than 4 in. (10 cm). This ant- and termite-eating snake looks like a worm.

Amphibians

In between fish and land vertebrates are amphibians, which develop lungs by the time they reach adulthood. But they can also breathe through their skin and the mucous membrane of their mouth, enabling them to live both in and out of the water.

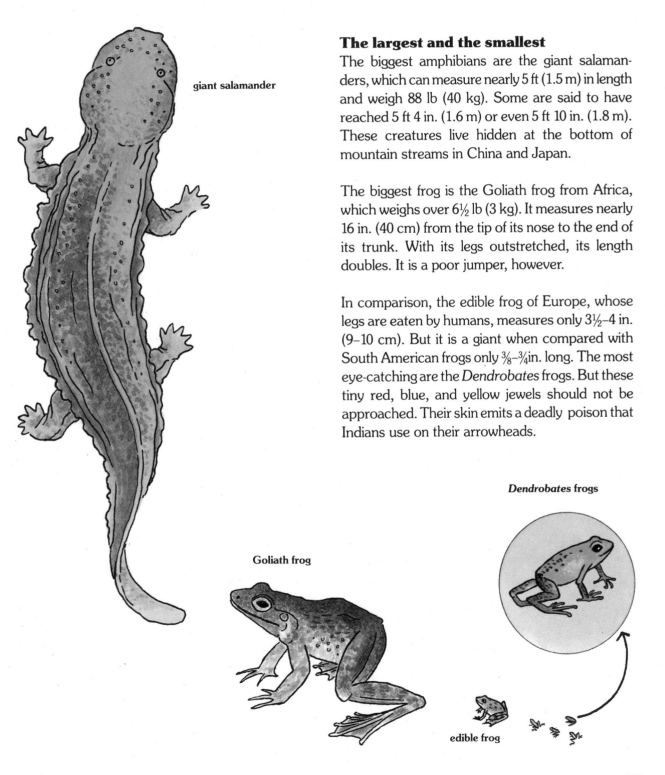

giant salamander

The largest and the smallest

The biggest amphibians are the giant salamanders, which can measure nearly 5 ft (1.5 m) in length and weigh 88 lb (40 kg). Some are said to have reached 5 ft 4 in. (1.6 m) or even 5 ft 10 in. (1.8 m). These creatures live hidden at the bottom of mountain streams in China and Japan.

The biggest frog is the Goliath frog from Africa, which weighs over 6½ lb (3 kg). It measures nearly 16 in. (40 cm) from the tip of its nose to the end of its trunk. With its legs outstretched, its length doubles. It is a poor jumper, however.

In comparison, the edible frog of Europe, whose legs are eaten by humans, measures only 3½–4 in. (9–10 cm). But it is a giant when compared with South American frogs only ⅜–¾ in. long. The most eye-catching are the *Dendrobates* frogs. But these tiny red, blue, and yellow jewels should not be approached. Their skin emits a deadly poison that Indians use on their arrowheads.

Dendrobates frogs

Goliath frog

edible frog

25

Fishes

To take a look at fishes, we leave solid ground and dive beneath the water. With more than 21,500 species—more than half the total vertebrate species—fish offer a wide variety of sizes, shapes, and colors...from the whale shark at 44,000 lb (20,000 kg) to a tiny goby at 0.00007 oz (0.002 g).

whale shark

The biggest fish in the world...

The biggest fishes belong to the shark family. The whale shark is the biggest of all. It weighs 22 tons (20 tonnes) and can measure up to 59 ft (18 m) long—some people say 75½ ft (23 m). Despite its

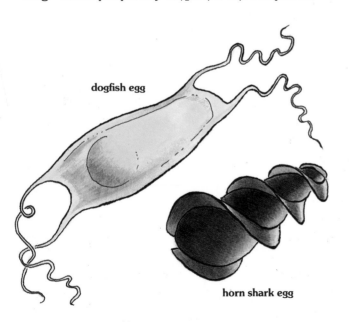

dogfish egg

horn shark egg

huge mouth with 310 rows of tiny teeth, this monster is harmless to humans. The whale shark feeds only on plankton and small fish, swallowing them while swimming slowly with its mouth open. It is believed that during feeding time, this shark filters about 528,000 gal (2 million l) of water every hour. Divers can get close to the whale shark without being in danger. They can even walk on the sandpaperlike 4-in. (10-cm) thick skin of its back.

and the biggest egg

The whale shark lays the biggest egg in the world, a rectangular case 14 x 12 x 3½ in.(36 x 30 x 9 cm). Its volume is that of 160 chicken eggs and more than 6 ostrich eggs. This egg is of the same kind as that laid by dogfishes, small sharks commonly found along the coast.

Other egg cases, such as that of the horn shark, are coiled up in a spiral. The females lay them in the cracks of rocks. In order to dislodge them, someone literally has to unscrew them.

Other giants

Although its size is more modest, the white shark—at nearly 40 ft (12 m) and 3.3 tons (3 tonnes)—is much more dangerous than its peaceful cousin. Its immense jaws, with several rows of teeth as sharp as razor blades, are feared by the biggest fish—and by bathers. Some beaches in Australia and South Africa have been surrounded by nets in order to protect swimmers from this huge predator.

The oarfish, nicknamed "king of the herrings," is a ribbonlike fish that can grow to 49 ft (15 m). Some people think it has inspired the legends of sea serpents. Its nickname comes from a story about the oarfish taking the lead during herring and salmon migrations, somewhat like a king leading an army of his subjects.

The manta ray, or giant devil ray, is the largest of all mantas. It is over 26 ft (8 m) wide and weighs 3.3 tons (3 tonnes). Mantas are thought to be ovoviviparous—giving birth to live young—and doing so during a gigantic leap out of the water. Then the newborn manta spreads its fins and glides into the water along with its mother.

The ocean sunfish can be 13 ft (4 m) across and weigh 2.2 tons (2 tonnes). This lazy-looking fish looks like a big flat head with no body, but actually it has a very small brain. The female lays 300 million eggs from which emerge fish the size of a pinhead, but relatively few survive, so the fish is rare.

The swordfish measures up to 16½ ft (5 m), including its "sword," which is more than 3 ft (1 m) long.

The opah is a brightly colored fish 6½ ft (2 m) long.

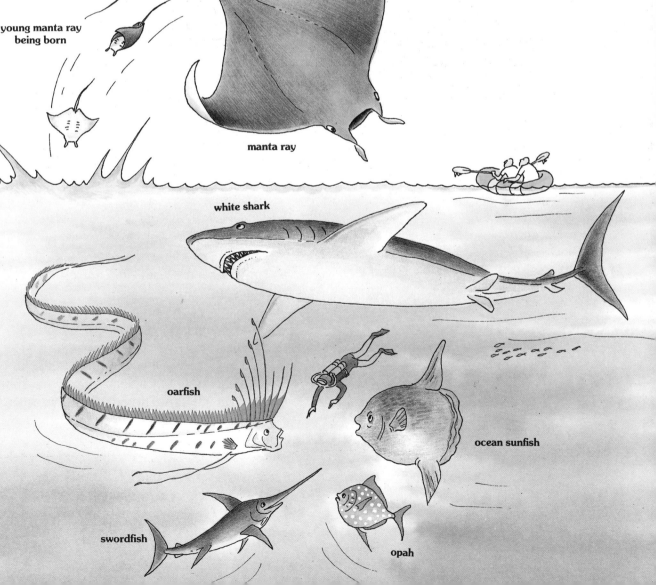

young manta ray being born

manta ray

white shark

oarfish

ocean sunfish

swordfish

opah

The biggest freshwater fishes

The Russian sturgeon can measure 29½ ft (9 m) length and weigh 1.5 tons (1.4 tonnes). It is the biggest fish one can meet in a river, where it lays its eggs in the summer. The rest of the year it lives in the Caspian and Black seas. One female can produce 220 lb (100 kg) of caviar (salted fish eggs, or roe), but it is not of top quality.

The wels, or European catfish, is a carnivorous freshwater fish that feeds on other fish, frogs, and even birds. It reaches a length of 16½ ft (5 m) and a weight of 660 lb (300 kg).

Russian sturgeon

wels, or European catfish

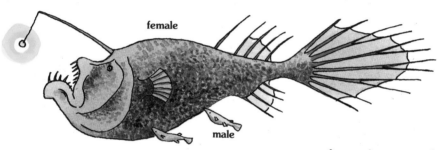

female

male

Ceratias hollbolli

Amazing couple

The difference in size between males and females reaches unusal lengths in a type of ceratiid angler, *Ceratias hollbolli*. The male is so small (2⅜ in., or 6 cm) that he lives with his mouth fixed on the body of the female, which measure about 4 ft (120 cm). Sometimes more than one male clings to the same female.

dwarf pygmy goby actual size

dwarf pygmy goby
enlarged 5 times

Tiniest

The smallest fishes—in fact, the smallest vertebrates—belong to the goby family. The tiniest, measuring less than ⅜ in. (9 mm), has been found recently in the Indian Ocean. The previous record was held by the dwarf pygmy goby from the Philippines, which measured 7/16 in. (11 mm). The dwarf pygmy goby lives in rivers but reproduces in the sea, where it can be caught by the billions. Fifteen thousand of them weigh only a pound.

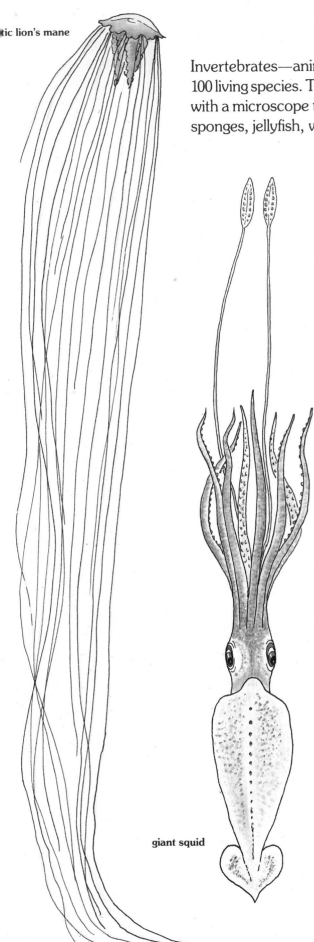
tic lion's mane

giant squid

Invertebrates

Invertebrates—animals without backbones—make up 97 out of every 100 living species. They range from one-celled animals you can see only with a microscope to giant creatures of the land and sea. They include sponges, jellyfish, worms, crustaceans, mollusks, and insects.

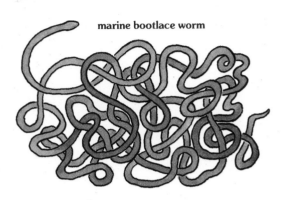
marine bootlace worm

The longest animal in the world
This record may be held by the marine bootlace worm. Although it is only about ⅜ in. (1 cm) wide on the average, some examples may reach a length of 180 ft (55 m). Since it is so hard to measure this worm—in nature it lies all tangled up like a plate of spaghetti—some scientists credit it with a length of only 98 feet (30 m).

A giant jellyfish
The biggest jellyfish is the Arctic lion's mane, whose thin tentacles can be as long as 131 ft (40 m). From its corolla, or "body," which measures 6½ ft (2 m) across, hang 1,200 poisonous tentacles. These form a net more than 5,000 sq ft (about 500 sq m) in size, in which the jellyfish catches shrimp and small fish. The tentacles can shrink to one-tenth of their normal size in only a second.

Boneless but heavy
The heaviest invertebrate is the giant squid. One of these, caught off New Zealand in 1933, measured 72 ft (22 m) long and weighed 6,600 lb (3,000 kg). Sperm whales like to eat the giant squid, but sometimes the squid can successfully fight off this predator.

Some big marine invertebrates

1. Giant barrel sponge: up to 5 ft 10 in. (1.8 m) high
2. Rhyzostome jellyfish: diameter of umbrella up to 3 ft (90 cm)
3. Ceriantharid: up to 6 ft 7 in. (2 m) long
4. Sea anemone: up to 2 ft (60 cm) high
5. Brain coral: up to 6 ft 1 in. (185 cm) across
6. Conch shell, largest gastropod: shell measures up to 27½ in. (70 cm) in length
7. Giant clam, largest bivalve mollusk: up to 59 in. across; weight more than 440 lb (200 kg)

8. Giant octopus: up to 23 ft (7 m) from tip of a tentacle to tip of opposite tentacle; weight up to 110 lb (50 kg)
9. Brisingidae starfish: up to 51 in. (130 cm) across; central disk less than 1¼ in. (3 cm)
10. Spiny starfish, biggest European starfish: up to 39 in. (10 m) across
11. Sunflower starfish: up to 35½ in. (90 cm)
12. Japanese giant spider crab, biggest crustacean: leg spread up to 11¾ ft (360 cm); weight to 40 lb (about 18 kg)

Longest land invertebrates

Giant earthworms hold this record, one from Australia (*Megascolides australis*) and the other from South Africa (*Microchaetus*). *Megascolides* is reported to grow to over 13 ft (4 m), but

earthworm
Microchaetus

Microchaetus is even larger—22 ft (6.7 m) or even 49 ft (15 m). Since the worm is so elastic, it is hard to get an exact measure. Its length changes when it stretches out and contracts.

Giant parasite

The longest parasite (living thing that lives off another living thing) is the broad fish tapeworm. It can be nearly 66 ft (20 m) long, with up to 4,000 segments. This horror can settle in the intestines of careless fish eaters—otters, cats, humans!

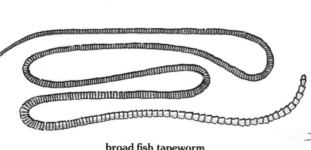

broad fish tapeworm

Big snail, little snail

The largest land snail is the giant African snail *Achatina achatina*. It weighs about 2 lb (almost 1 kg), and its shell measures up to 1 ft (30 cm) long. People have foolishly introduced this snail to Asia and America, where it causes great plant damage. Compare it in size to the edible snail and the garden snail.

The smallest land snail, *Palaina obesa*, from New Caledonia, is not visible in the illustration on this page since it measures only 1/25 in. (1 mm) when adult.

garden snail

edible snail

Achatina achatina

The biggest spiders

These are the therasophids from Brazil, called "bird-eating" spiders because they supposedly eat small birds. The biggest ones have a legspan of 10½ in. (27 cm), a body of 3½ in. (9 cm), and a weight of 2¾ oz (80 g). They eat frogs and small poisonous snakes, too.

bird-eating spider

Invisible

The smallest living beings are the protozoans, made up of only one cell. Most of them can be seen only through a microscope. Their sizes vary from as much as 0.2 in. for the trumpet-shaped stentors to less than 1/25,000 in. (less than a micron—1/1,000 mm) for such disease-spreading parasites as the *Leishmania*.

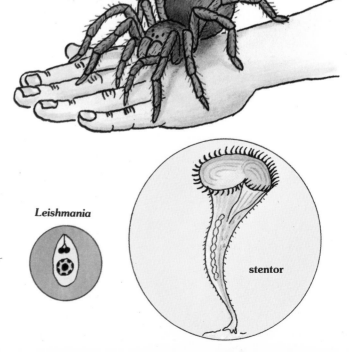

Leishmania

stentor

Insects

Insects, like crustaceans and spiders, are invertebrates. Because of their huge numbers— more than 750,000 species—and their presence in our lives, we will look at them separately.

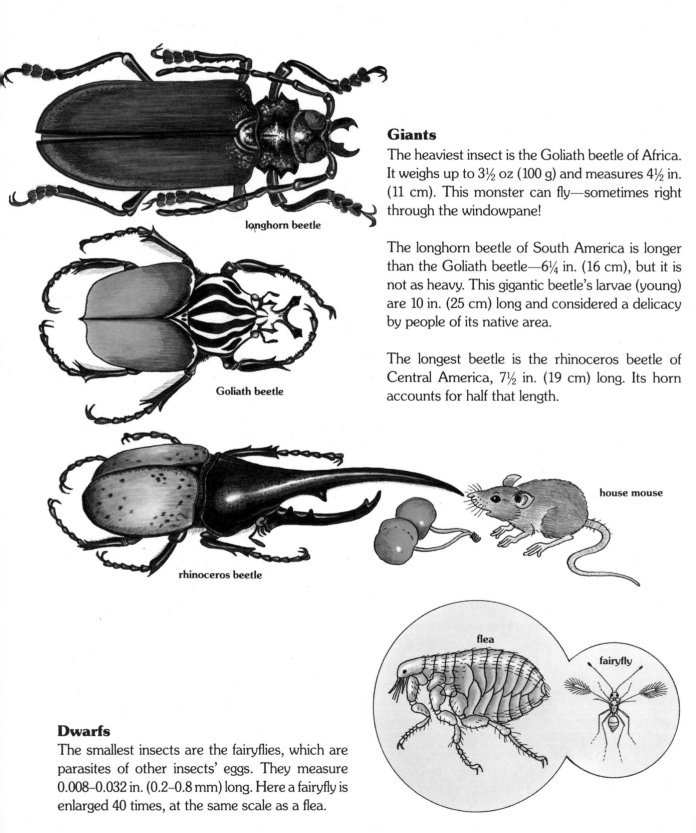

longhorn beetle

Goliath beetle

rhinoceros beetle

house mouse

flea

fairyfly

Giants

The heaviest insect is the Goliath beetle of Africa. It weighs up to 3½ oz (100 g) and measures 4½ in. (11 cm). This monster can fly—sometimes right through the windowpane!

The longhorn beetle of South America is longer than the Goliath beetle—6¼ in. (16 cm), but it is not as heavy. This gigantic beetle's larvae (young) are 10 in. (25 cm) long and considered a delicacy by people of its native area.

The longest beetle is the rhinoceros beetle of Central America, 7½ in. (19 cm) long. Its horn accounts for half that length.

Dwarfs

The smallest insects are the fairyflies, which are parasites of other insects' eggs. They measure 0.008–0.032 in. (0.2–0.8 mm) long. Here a fairyfly is enlarged 40 times, at the same scale as a flea.

The biggest butterflies and moths—lepidoptera

The biggest butterfly active by day is the Queen Alexandra birdwing of the Solomon Islands. Its wingspan is 10¼ in. (26 cm).

The moth with the greatest wing surface is the giant silkworm moth of Australia, with a wingspan of almost 10 in. (25 cm) and a wing surface of 46½ sq in. (300 sq cm).

The lepidopteran with the greatest wingspan—12 in. (30 cm)—is the great owlet moth from Central and South America. It is active at night.

Brooke's birdwing, from India and Australia, has a wingspan of almost 10 in. (25 cm).

Morpho rhetenor from Brazil, has a wingspan of 5 in. (12 cm).

Queen Alexandra birdwing

giant silkworm moth

great owlet moth

Brooke's birdwing

Morpho rhetenor

The smallest lepidopteran

The English moth *Johanssonia acetosa* has a wingspan no larger than 0.08 in. (2 mm).

Long but invisible

The longest insects belong to the phasma family. They are mimetic—champions at imitating sticks or leaves. In the daytime they stay motionless and blend in with the bushes where they hide. The longest of these insects, *Pharnacia serratipes* of Malaysia, measures 13 in. (33 cm) from its head to the tip of its abdomen. It is harmless and eats only leaves.

The larva of *Pharnacia serratipes* is a little over 1 in. (3 cm) long and without legs when it comes out, all wrinkled, from an egg measuring 0.12 in. x 0.20 in. (3 mm x 5 mm). (On pages 34–35, the adult insect is drawn to its actual size.)

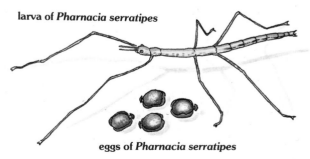

larva of *Pharnacia serratipes*

eggs of *Pharnacia serratipes*

Hummingbirds and phasmas

PHASMAS
1. *Pharnacia serratipes* 13 in. (33 cm)
2. *Extatosoma goliath* 12 in. (30 cm)
3. *Eurycnema herculeana* 9 in. (22 cm)
4. *Extatosoma tiaratum* 6 in. (15 cm)
5. *Phyllium crurifolium* 3 in. (8 cm)

OTHER MIMETIC INSECTS
6. *Congulus congylides*
7. *Umbonia spinosa*
8. *Hypsauchenia hardwigii*

HUMMINGBIRDS
9. Bee hummingbird 0.05 oz (1.6 g)
10. Vervain hummingbird 0.07 oz (2
11. Amethyst woodstar 0.11 oz (3 g
12. Frilled coquette 0.11 oz (3 g)
13. Ruby-throated hummingbird
14. Ruby-topaz hummingbird
15. Marvelous spatuletail
    Weights for 13, 14, and 15 not
    confirmed.

This illustration compares
the actual sizes of phasmas
and hummingbirds. In real life you
would not see them side by side. Phasmas
live in tropical Asia, while hummingbirds live in North,
Central, and South America.

CONCLUSION

We have taken a brief look at the amazing size differences among the world's animals. Enormous blue whales swim alongside microscopic creatures. Tiny insects live on huge elephants. Sometimes an animal, such as a small fish, can have an incredibly long tapeworm living *inside* it!

People have learned much about the roles that animals—large and small—play in nature. Scientists have come to see that an animal's importance to the balance of life on earth does not necessarily depend on its size.

INDEX OF NAMES

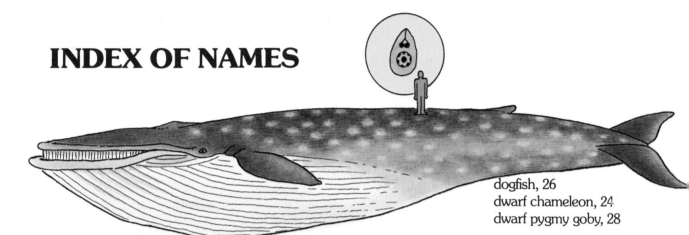